BUTTER

Susan Wake

Illustrations by John Yates

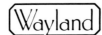

Food

Apples	**Herbs and spices**
Beans and pulses	**Meat**
Bread	**Milk**
Butter	**Pasta**
Cakes and biscuits	**Potatoes**
Cheese	**Rice**
Citrus fruit	**Sugar**
Eggs	**Tea**
Fish	**Vegetables**

All words that appear in **bold** are explained in the glossary on page 30.

Editor: Heather Ancient

First published in 1989 by Wayland (Publishers) Limited
61 Western Road, Hove, East Sussex BN3 1JD, England.

© Copyright 1989 Wayland (Publishers) Limited

British Library Cataloguing in Publication Data
Wake, Susan
    Butter.
    1. Butter – For children
    I. Title   II. Series
    641.3'72

Typeset by Kalligraphics Ltd., Horley, Surrey
Printed in Italy by G. Canale & C.S.p.A., Turin
Bound by Casterman S.A., Belgium

Contents

A natural food

The butter we put on our food is made from cows' milk.

Butter has been an important part of our diet for thousands of years. It is even mentioned in the Bible.

Butter is made from the butterfat in cream. It is a natural food product and no artificial flavours, colours or **preservatives** may be added to it.

There are two main kinds of butter. These are

known as sweet cream and lactic. Sweet cream butter is made from pure cream. It is produced in Britain, New Zealand and some parts of Europe.

Lactic butter is made by adding specially selected **bacteria** to the cream. The bacteria make the cream slightly sour and give the butter a stronger taste. Lactic butter is made in European countries like Holland, Denmark and France.

Butter in the past

fleeter

setting dish

plunger

In the past, people learnt how to get milk from animals like cows, goats, sheep and even camels. They soon found that milk went sour quickly so they learnt how to make other products from it, like yoghurt, cheese and butter.

No one knows when butter was first made. It may have been made by accident. Perhaps someone carrying milk on horseback found that after the milk had been jogged for a while there

wooden iron-bound churn

wooden churn

were little lumps of fat in it.

To make butter the milk was left to stand overnight so the cream containing the butterfat floated to the top. This cream was skimmed off into a churn and shaken (churned). Churning made the fat separate from the liquid. The fat formed globules (small drops) which stuck together and made grains of butter. The liquid which was left, the buttermilk, was poured off. Then the butter was washed with cold water and kneaded to remove air bubbles. Finally the butter was moulded into shape.

Special tools were needed for making butter in the past.

Scotch hands

glass churn

butter worker

7

Many farms used wooden butter-moulds which had a picture carved inside. This picture often showed what type of farm the butter had come from – so corn sheaves meant a corn-growing farm and a swan meant a farm with water meadows. When the butter was finished it was taken to market to be sold.

The dairy was a special cool room where the milk was kept and butter and cheese were made.

Butter from farms was sold at markets. It was cut and weighed in the open air.

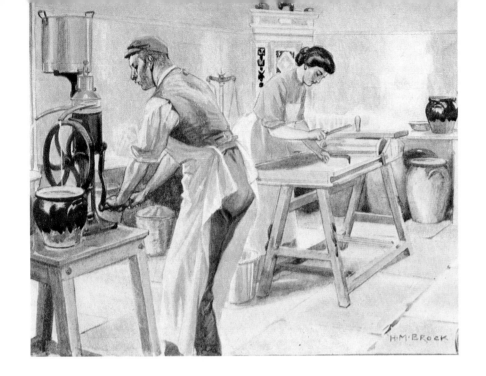

Left *Butter-making in the dairy. The machine the man is using separates the cream from the milk.*

Below *A Bedouin woman using an animal-skin bag to churn cream.*

Butter was mainly made by women, known as dairy maids.

Sometimes the cream would not churn and the dairy maids thought a witch or fairies had cast a spell on it. It was more likely that the temperature was wrong because if cream is too cold it takes a long time to churn. A common cure was to put a red-hot poker into the cream. This was supposed to burn the witch but as it raised the temperature it did often help to make the butter.

Butter today

The continuous method of butter-making. After the cream is churned the butter is pushed out in a long strip.

The basic way of producing butter is the same today as it was when it was first made. Few places still use the old methods of churning by hand, though. Today's modern **creameries** use machinery which can make butter in one continuous process. Cream is fed in at one end of the machinery and butter comes out at the other.

To collect the cream, milk is heated and fed into a high-powered machine, called a separator. This is spun very quickly (6,000 times a minute). The cream collects in the middle because it is lighter than the skimmed milk which is flung outwards. The cream and skimmed milk flow out of the separator down different pipes.

If lactic butter is being made, the cream is now soured slightly. Then the cream for both types of butter is **pasteurized.**

The pasteurized cream now passes into a

The butter is cut into blocks and wrapped by the machine.

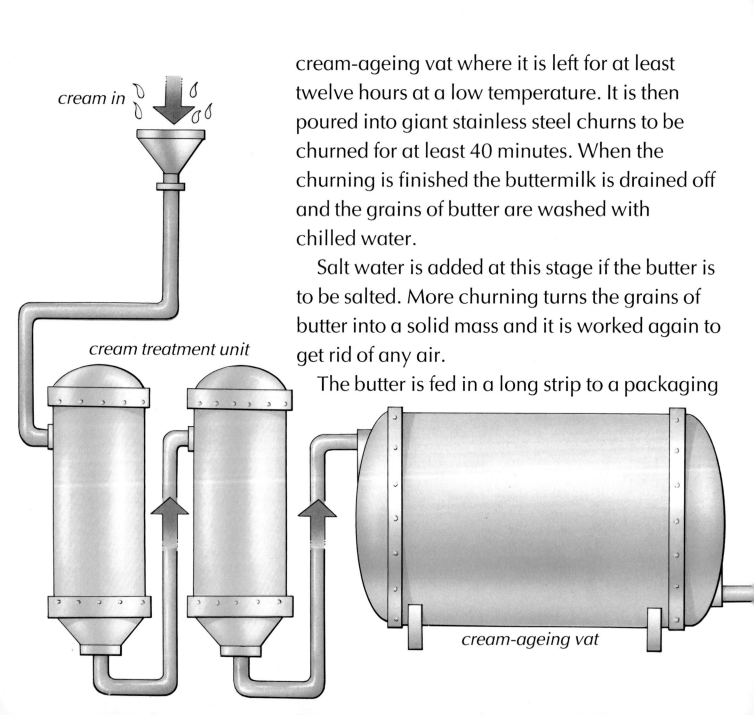

cream in

cream treatment unit

cream-ageing vat

cream-ageing vat where it is left for at least twelve hours at a low temperature. It is then poured into giant stainless steel churns to be churned for at least 40 minutes. When the churning is finished the buttermilk is drained off and the grains of butter are washed with chilled water.

Salt water is added at this stage if the butter is to be salted. More churning turns the grains of butter into a solid mass and it is worked again to get rid of any air.

The butter is fed in a long strip to a packaging

machine. Here it is cut and wrapped. The weight of the packs is checked and then they are packed into boxes ready for delivery to **wholesalers** and then on to shops.

Hygiene is very important in the production process and all the equipment must be free from bacteria and germs. Samples are regularly tested to ensure that they are of the highest possible quality. The packs of butter are stamped with sell-by dates so that we can tell when the butter is at its best.

This diagram shows how butter is made in one continuous process in a modern creamery.

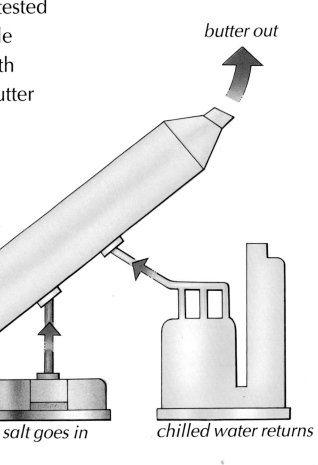

butter out

chilled water

churning

buttermilk

salt goes in

chilled water returns

The food in butter

Butter and margarine contain fat which our bodies turn into energy. They are also a good source of **vitamins** A and D. Vitamin A is important for good vision, for growth and for healthy skin. Vitamin D is needed to help build our bones and teeth.

Butter has always been regarded as an important part of a healthy diet and all dairy

Butter adds flavour to many foods but eating too much fat can affect your health.

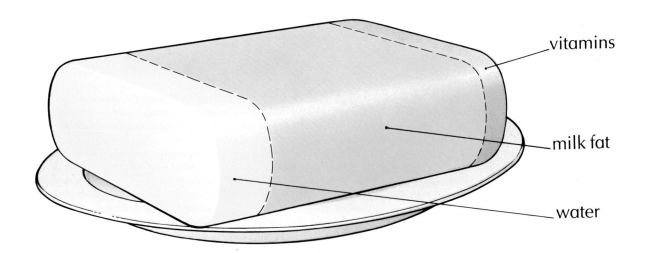

vitamins

milk fat

water

products were thought to be good for us. But now health experts are not so sure. Rich milk and butter contain a large amount of a substance called **cholesterol.** Too much of this in our diet can clog up the **arteries** which carry blood around our bodies. This can lead to heart disease.

The dairy industries say that the goodness in dairy products outweighs the possible dangers to our health from cholesterol. However, we must be careful that we choose a balanced diet and do not have too much of any one type of food.

This diagram shows the different amounts of nutrients in butter.

15

Make your own butter

It is simple to make your own butter but it takes quite a lot of shaking and can make your arms ache so you may need some friends to help you.

You will need: A small, clear screw top jar, single cream (or the top of the milk) – enough to half fill the jar.

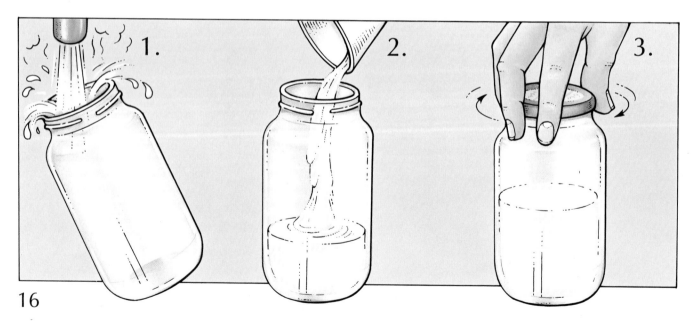

1.

2.

3.

1. Wash the jar thoroughly with hot water.
2. Pour in the cream.
3. Screw the top on tightly.
4. Shake, shake, shake . . .
5. After a while you will notice that the cream separates into a liquid (buttermilk) and solid grains of butter.
6. Continue to shake until the grains become a solid mass of butter. Pour off the buttermilk and try the butter that you have made.

You can drink the buttermilk left from your butter-making.

17

Margarine

Margarine became an important substitute for butter. Many margarine factories, like this one in Frankfurt in Germany, were opened.

Margarine was invented just over 100 years ago when the number of people in France had grown very quickly. There were more people than ever to feed and butter was becoming **scarce.** The

Emperor, Napoleon III, offered a prize for the invention of a **substitute** for butter.

Margarine was invented by a chemist called Hippolyte Mège Mouriès.

Mège Mouriès made margarine by softening beef fat and mixing it with salty water and milk. The Dutch were the first people to produce

Margarine is made from oils which are hardened, coloured and flavoured to make blocks of fat which look like butter.

19

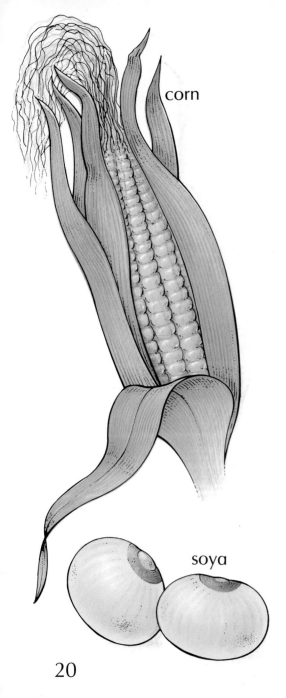
corn

margarine but factories quickly opened in other parts of Europe and the USA. At first the flavour was not very good and it lacked vitamins but people were grateful to have any substitute for butter. Margarine was cheaper than butter, too.

When beef fat became expensive, the people making margarine had to find other fats to use. They tried vegetable oils but these were too liquid. However, by the early 1900s they found a way to make vegetable oil harder. They also

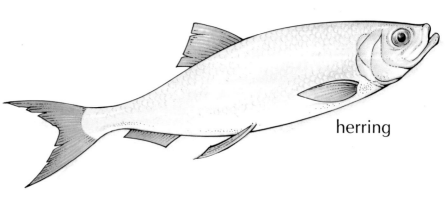
herring

soya

learnt how to remove the taste from oils. This meant they could then get fats for margarine from many sources – both plant and animal.

Vitamins could be added, too, and margarine became just as good as butter. Today there are many varieties. Some margarines are sold in blocks like butter, others are soft and ready for spreading. Some margarines are specially made so they contain less fat. Most margarines have added colour, flavourings and preservatives.

coconut

peanuts

pilchard

sunflower 21

Butter or margarine?

Try to design a test to see if people can tell the difference between butter and margarine.

Make a list of the things that you will need and the things that you must do.

Remember
Keep the spreads in unmarked containers.
Make sure that *you* know which is which.
Spread both butter and margarine on to the same

For the first part of the test, put a little bit of butter and margarine in separate unmarked dishes.

Left Spread bread and crackers with the margarine and butter.

food (bread or crackers).

Spread equal amounts on.

Ask people to try both and tell you which is butter.

Record your results on paper and at the end of the test produce a bar chart.

Can you draw any **conclusions** from your results?
If you had to design this test again what would you do differently?
Ask someone to test you.
Did you get it right?

Below Can you tell the difference?

Butter in the kitchen

Butter has many and varied uses. It can be eaten as a spread on food like bread, biscuits, scones or muffins. It is also a basic **ingredient** in many recipes, such as cakes, biscuits, pastry, puddings and sauces.

Butter can be used to add flavour to vegetables as when served on hot baked potatoes. It is also often used for frying and grilling. Many people, especially Asians, use butter which has been clarified. This is butter which is melted and the solids which come to the surface are skimmed off. It is also called ghee.

Butter is usually sold in blocks but can be made into small pats, balls, curls or cubes.

To keep it at its best, butter should be stored in a cool, dark place away from strong smells. It can be frozen but it will keep fresh in the refrigerator for several weeks. Butter which is going bad will taste and smell very sour.

Butter can be used to make table decorations like this beautiful swan.

Savoury butters

These are highly seasoned butters which add flavour to many dishes. After making them they should be well chilled, cut into small 'pats' of ½ cm thickness and put on to hot food immediately before serving.

Curry butter

You will need:

50g butter
1 level teaspoon of curry powder
¼ level teaspoon of turmeric
1 teaspoon of lemon juice

1. Cream the butter until it is soft.

2. Beat in the remaining ingredients.

3. Chill.

Garlic butter

You will need:

2 garlic cloves
50g butter

3. Cream the butter until it is soft.

1. Peel the garlic and boil in a little water for about 5 minutes.

4. Gradually beat in the garlic.

2. Drain and chop very finely.

5. Chill.

Bread and butter pudding

You will need, for 4 people:

6 thin slices of bread
50g butter
50g currants or sultanas
2 large eggs
40g caster sugar
600 ml milk

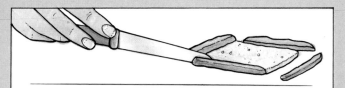

1. Cut the crusts off the bread. Spread the slices with butter.

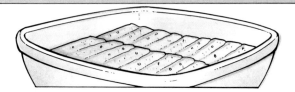

2. Cut into fingers and put half of them into a greased 1 litre heat-proof dish.

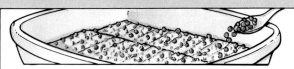

3. Sprinkle with the fruit and half of the sugar.

4. Top with the remaining bread (buttered side up). Sprinkle with the rest of the sugar.

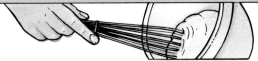

5. Beat the eggs and milk together. Pour over the bread. Leave to stand for 30 minutes.

6. Bake in the centre of the oven at 160°C, 325°F, gas mark 3 for 45 minutes to 1 hour or until the pudding is set and the top is crisp and golden.

Cheesy biscuits

(makes about 30 biscuits)

You will need:

50g butter
50g soft cheese
½ an egg yolk
pinch of salt
¼ teaspoon of paprika
50g sifted flour

1. Cream the butter until it is fluffy.

2. Gradually beat in the cheese, egg, salt and paprika.

3. Fold in the flour until the mixture forms a dough. Chill in the refrigerator for 1 hour.

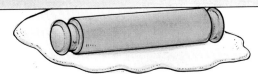

4. Knead the dough for 3 minutes, then roll out to about ¾ cm thick.

5. Cut into small circles with a pastry cutter.

6. Put the circles on a lightly greased baking sheet. Cook for 10 minutes or until browned at 425°F, 220°C, gas mark 7.

29

Glossary

Arteries Blood vessels carrying blood from the heart.

Bacteria Tiny living organisms present everywhere. Some can cause disease. When they settle on food they increase rapidly and gradually destroy the food.

Cholesterol A white soapy substance which exists in large quantities in animal fats. It can coat the walls of arteries making them narrower and making it harder for blood to pass through.

Conclusions Decisions arising from information gathered.

Creameries Factories where cream, cheese and butter are made.

Hygiene Cleanliness.

Ingredient One of the materials in a mixture.

Pasteurized Heated to 70°C (158°F) for 15 seconds and then cooled quickly to kill harmful bacteria.

Preservatives Chemicals that slow the decay of food.

Scarce Difficult to obtain.

Substitute To use instead of something else.

Vitamins Substances found in food which we need to keep us healthy and help us grow.

Wholesalers People who buy things in large quantities to sell on to shops or markets.

Books to read

Butter and Margarine by Lorna Hinds (Franklin Watts, 1982)

Dairy Farming by Geoffrey Patterson (André Deutsch, 1983)

Focus on Dairy Produce by Richard Clarke (Wayland, 1985)

Food in History by Sheila Robertson (Wayland, 1983)

Health and Food by Dorothy Baldwin (Wayland, 1987)

Milk by Dorothy Turner (Wayland, 1988)

Index

Picture acknowledgements

The photographs in this book were provided by: Mary Evans Picture Library 8, 9 (top), 18; Milk Marketing Board 10, 11; Christine Osborne/Middle East Pictures 9 (bottom), 14, 19; Paul Seheult 22, 23; Topham Picture Library 25.